MW01290924

SAT

TIPS

CHEATS & TRICKS

The Ultimate

1 Hour

SAT Prep Course

Basic Tips

Your Guess is as Good as Mine!

If you can eliminate even just one wrong answer, guess! Since you only lose ¼ point for a wrong answer, the more you guess the better the chance you will get one correct.

General

Clueless?

If you have absolutely
<u>no clue</u> to the answer,
do not guess!

<u>Skip It</u>.

Easy Does It!

Answer the easy questions first! Spend most of your time on the questions in the beginning of a section ... they are easier!

General

Fuhgetaboutit!

Skip the hard questions! If you know you are going to probably skip some questions, make sure they are the (hardest) last questions in the section.

General

F This!

In school, a 50% is a failing grade. On the SAT however 50% is not bad! If you only answer half the questions on the SAT correctly and leave the rest blank your score would be….520 on critical reading 520 Math and 500 on writing.

General

Come Back Later

Circle questions you want to come back to later, and mark an X for questions you want to skip entirely.

General

About The Test

3 Hours 45 Minutes

10 Sections

Critical Reading

3 Sections 70 Minutes

Math

3 Sections 70 Minutes

Writing

3 Sections 60 Minutes

Variable

1 Section 25 Minutes (Not Scored)

General

Critical
Reading Tips

Sentence Completions

&

Reading Passages

Use Your Words!

Put your own word in the blank before you even look at the answers ... then match your word to the best answer.

Sentence Completions

Blankity Blank!

If the question has <u>two blanks</u> try matching the <u>second</u> blank first … some of the first blanks are similar in meaning.

Sentence Completions

Go Easy Early!

If the question is early in the section ... the answer is probably an obvious easy word.

If question is in the last half of the section ... the answer is probably a hard word.

Sentence Completion

Are you Positive?

Read the sentence and decide whether the blank (or blanks) should be positive or negative. Write the sign in the blank. Then check the words and determine which ones fit. Cross out the ones that don't work.

Sentence Completion

Politically Correct!

If the passage or sentence completion has to do with women or minorities....the answer will almost always paint them in a positive light.

Sentence Completion & Passages

Underline!

If you chose to read the passage first, <u>underline key phrases or nouns as you read</u>. As you answer the questions you can refer back to your underlines.

Passages

First Things First!

When comparing two passages … the question will refer you to a line or passage number ... answer the questions about the **first passage first**.   Then, answer the ones about the second passage. Finally, answer the rest.

Passages

Pretend you care!

If you pretend you are interested in the passage you will do better. Your brain does not remember things that it finds boring.

Passages

Not So Smarty Pants!

Beware of the answers that sound too intelligent.....they are usually wrong. The right answer is usually the one that is most <u>basic and simple</u>.

Passages

Read the Questions first.

If you quickly skim the questions first....you will have an Idea of what you need to know when you read the passage. When you go back to read the passage... circle phrases that answer the questions you read.

Passages

Way Too Long

If you are running out of time on the subsections....skip the final and longest reading passage...it takes too much time.

Passages

Absolutely Wrong!

If the answer states an <u>absolute</u> or <u>definite</u> point of view it is usually <u>wrong</u>. Cross it out.

Passages

Beware!!!

If you see the following words or phrases in the answer it is probably **WRONG:**

Always, Extremely, Must, Never ,Could Only, Undoubtedly, Fully

Passages

Wishy Washy is Wonderful

If you see the following words or phrases the answer is probably **CORRECT.**

Could Be, May Be, Might Be, Minorly, Suggests, Implies, Could Be Seen As, Arguably

Passages

Pickup Lines!

If the question refers to a line number….the answer is somewhere between <u>4 lines above it</u> or <u>4 lines below it</u> … forget the rest of the passage.

Passages

No Line!

If the question doesn't give you a line number … the answer is in the <u>first few lines</u> … or the <u>last few lines</u> of the passage!

Passages

Primary Purpose!

If the question asks you about the author's "Primary Purpose" … the answer is in the <u>first few lines</u> of the passage … or <u>the last few lines</u>.

Passages

When In Rome

If you see a question with Roman Numerals, and you don't know the answer, <u>guess the Roman Numeral that shows up **most** in the answers</u>.

Example:

Which of the following is true?

    (A)   I only
    (B)   II only
    (C)   I and II only
    (D)   I and III only
    (E)   I, II and III

Since (I) shows up 4 times, you should choose (A). If you think there is also another answer, choose (C) because (II) shows up 3 times.

Don't Bother!

Don't read the example problems...they are a waste of your time. You should know the directions beforehand.

Read The Intro!

Always read the intro to a passage … it will help you understand what you are about to read and identify people or definitions that you need to know.

Passages

Droppin' Science

There will always be a Scientific Passage. You do not need to understand scientific terms to answer the questions about the passage. The sentence before or after the term you don't understand usually explains it.

Passages

History Is No Mystery

If there is a historical passage, underline the names of historians who might agree or disagree with the author. There will probably be a question about them.

Passages

Art Is Good

If there is a passage about Art, it will usually be positive. The answers will usually be complimentary towards whoever or whatever type of art is discussed.

Note: "Art" can refer to painting, sculpture, literature, music or craft; or a particular artist, musician or writer.

Passages

The Giant Passage

Because it is so big, the questions tend to follow the order in which the answers appear in the passage. The first questions are about the early parts of the passage. The middle questions are about the middle part of the passage. The last questions are about the last part of the passage.

Passages

Quick Fix!

Prefixes: If a word starts with the following prefix, it can help you decode words you don't know.

Prefix	Meaning
A	Without
Ante	Before
Anti	Against
Auto	Self
Bene	Good

Prefix	Meaning
Bi	Two
Circum	Around
Contra	Against
Di	Two
Dict	Speak
Dis	Apart
Homo	Same
Hyper	Above
Hypo	Below
Inter	Between

Prefix	Meaning
Mal	Bad
Micro	Small
Mis	Wrong
Multi	Many
Neo	New
Poly	Many
Pro	For
Re	Again
Retro	Back
Sanct	Holy

Math Tips

Easy Does It.

The Math questions go from easy to hard. Do the easy ones first

Math

Plug it In

If you don't know how to answer....plug in the answer to see if it works. Try answer "C" first.

Math

Don't waste your time

If you think a math problem is going to take you too much time … circle and skip it.   Come back later if you can.

Math

Mean Median Mode

The <u>Mean</u> is the average. Add up the numbers and divide by number of numbers.

The <u>Median</u> is the middle number. If there are an even number of numbers ... average the middle 2.

<u>The Mode</u> is the most frequently occurring number in a set.

Math

Bring It!

Bring a calculator. This may sound obvious … but don't forget it. Make sure it has fresh batteries and bring extras just in case.

Math

Don't Fear Factors!

Divisible By	If:
1	It's an integer
2	It's an even number
3	It's digits add up to multiples of 3
4	It's last two digits form number divisible by 4
5	It ends in 5 or 0
6	It is divisible by 2 and 3
7	No Rule
8	It's last 3 digits form a multiple of 8
9	It's digits add up to a multiple of 9
10	It ends in 0

Fair and Square

Remember these squares to save time in your calculations.

Number	Squared
11	121
12	144
13	169
14	196
15	225
16	256
17	289
18	324
19	361
20	400

Remember: 25 x25 = 625

Fractions

Don't change fractions to decimals during your calculations. It is not necessary.

Math

What's the Angle?

<u>Congruent</u> Angles

have the same number of degrees.

<u>Complementary</u>

Angles add up to 90 degrees

<u>Supplementary</u> Angles

add up 180 degrees

Parallelograms are shapes with opposite sides that are parallel. They have 2 pairs of equal angles.

Similar Triangles are two triangles with angles of the same measure in different sizes.

Triangles have angles that <u>ALWAYS add up to 90 degrees</u>

Area 51

Area of Rectangle = Length x Width

Area of Triangle = ½ Base x Height

Area of Circle = π x r^2 (r = radius)

Circle of Trust

Area of Circle $= \pi \times r^2$
(r = radius)

Circumference $= 2\pi \times r$

Volume

Length x Width x Height

Perpendiculous

Perpendicular means lines that intersect at right angles (90 degrees)

Off on a Tangent.

A line is Tangent to a circle if it makes a right angle with the circles radius and is outside the circle.

Math Grid-Ins

Good News! <u>You do not lose ANY points</u> if you get these questions wrong so <u>it's ok to guess</u> if you have no idea.

Math

Writing Tips

Sentence Errors and The Essay

Talk To Yourself.

Read the question quickly and listen for the error.

Something that sounds wrong probably is.

If you find an error, mark it down. If there is no error, mark the letter E

Sentence Errors

No A

Read the whole sentence not just the underlined part.

Never read choice A. Choice A is always the same as the original. Don't waste your time reading it again.

If there is no error, choose A.

Sentence Errors

The Shortest Cut

If you have NO IDEA, choose the SHORTEST answer. The simplest answer is usually correct.

Sentence Errors

Slanguage

Always <u>stay away from slang or clichés</u> when looking for answers, or when you are writing your essay.

Sentence Errors & Essay

<u>Being</u> Wrong

Stay away from answer choices that start with the word "Being." They are almost always wrong!

Example:

Being that these answers are always wrong, you should stay away from them.

Sentence Errors

Make it Up!

When writing your essay, if you do not have any evidence to support your point of view....MAKE IT UP! Just make sure that what you say is not obviously false.

Essay

It's Not What You Say

The reader does not care about what you say, but how well you say it! The essay is a test of your persuasive writing skills.

Essay

Size Matters

Be wordy on the essay. You are given 2 pages for your essay. Make sure you fill up the entire 2 pages.

Essay

One Shot!

The reader of your essay will only read it once. They are looking for a general understanding of essay structure, proper grammar and supporting details.

Essay

Do Me First

Sentence completions take the least amount of time. Do them first. Do the short reading passage next. Then do the long reading passages.

Plan Ahead

Write a general version of your essay before you take the test!   Write about something that interests you and that you understand. Fit your essay and knowledge to the question.

Essay

The Essay Prompt:
Answer Example Ideas

History References

The American Revolution: Tenacity, Courage

Martin Luther King: Courage, Sacrifice, Vision

Abraham Lincoln: Persistence, Self Made Man

Adolph Hitler: Corruption, Evil, Propaganda

Gandhi: Sacrifice, Courage,

Civil Rights Movement: Struggle, Achievement

<u>The Civil War</u>: Can be adapted to most prompts

Literature

<u>Catcher in the Rye</u>: Frustration, Change

<u>Julius Caesar</u>: Pride, Downfall, Revenge

<u>Brave New World</u>: Technology, Personal Freedom

<u>Frankenstein</u>: Dangerous Knowledge, Science, Rejection by Society

<u>The Scarlet Letter</u>: Sin, Identity

<u>The Outsiders</u>: Rich vs. Poor, Chaos

Write What You Know

Personal examples are good topics to reference. Anything you have experienced can be used to answer the prompt.

Essay

Fiction

If you are completely stumped, make up a foreign sounding author, human rights advocate or scientist. Then customize his or her life to fit the prompt.

Essay

Sparknotes Essay!

Before the test, go to Sparknotes.Com and look for books that you have read. Review the "Themes and Motifs" and study them. Use what you remember on the essay.

Essay

Essay Format

Paragraph 1: Introduction

1. State your position (Thesis)
2. Explain your examples.

Paragraph 2,3,4: Example 1,2,3

1. 4 to 5 sentences per paragraph (example)
2. First sentence should state your example
3. Support your thesis through facts.

Paragraph 5: Conclusion

1. Recap your argument
2. Look to the future

Final Tips

No Three in a Row

If you answer 2 questions in a row and the answer is C, the next question is <u>probably not</u> C. You need to be sure that the first two questions you answered are correct though. This trick is not foolproof. The third answer might be C.

No Answer

If one of the choices says "it cannot be determined from the information given," there is about a 50 percent chance that this answer is correct … only if it is offered at the beginning of a section. If it is offered at the end…then it is usually a trick and therefore incorrect.

Google It!

If you need more detailed tips about SAT tips and strategies, Google it! There are hundreds of people on Google who want nothing more than to prove how smart they are. Why not take advantage of their expertise?

Going 'Round In Circles

Don't waste time filling in circles. The quickest way to fill in the circle is from the inside out. Start in the middle and fill in the circle in a circular motion from inside out. This will give you more time to concentrate on the questions.

Scooby Snacks

Believe it or not, you are allowed to bring food to the SAT. Don't eat during the test though…it wastes time. Eat in between sections.

Dress for Success

Wear loose comfortable clothes. You want to be able to relax and concentrate. No one else cares what you look like. Everyone else is too worried about the test to even notice you.

Nail It!

Cut your nails so you don't waste time biting them during the test.

Watch It!

Wear a watch to the test. This will help you pace yourself and keep track of time.

Wear Earplugs.

If you are distracted easily, earplugs will help you concentrate. Silence will help you focus. All you will hear is the sound of yourself breathing and your heartbeat.

Vocabulary Word Bundles

Why memorize individual words when you can memorize groups of words that have similar meanings?

Feeling Superior

Arrogant, Braggart,
Complacent, Contemptuous,
Disdainful, Egotistical,
Haughty, Insolent,
Narcissistic, Ostentatious,
Presumptuous, Pretentious,
Supercilious, Swagger

Being Quiet or Using Few Words

Brevity, Concise, Laconic, Pithy, Quiescent, Reticent, Succinct, Taciturn, Terse

Dull & Unoriginal

Banal, Cliché, Derivative,
Hackneyed, Insipid,
Lackluster, Mundane,
Platitude, Prosaic, Trite, Vapid

Lacking Energy or Movement

Indolent, Languor, Lassitude, Lethargic, Sedentary, Sluggish, Soporific, Stagnant, Torpid

Being Careful

Chary, Circumspect,
Conscientious, Exacting,
Gingerly, Heedful, Meticulous,
Scrupulous, Vigilant, Wary

Puzzles, Problems & Disasters

Adversity, Conflagration,
Confounding, Cryptic,
Debacle, Enigma, Labyrinth,
Precarious, Quagmire,
Quandary, Turbulence,
Turmoil

More than Enough

Ample, Copious, Lavish,
Myriad, Plethora, Profuse,
Prolific, Superfluous, Surfeit

Scolding & Criticizing

Berate, Carp, Castigate,
Censure, Chastise, Deprecate,
Deride, Impugn, Rebuff,
Rebuke, Reprove, Upbraid

Old or New

Old: Antediluvian,
Antiquated, Antiquity,
Archaic, Obsolete, Relic

New: Contemporary,
Inception, Innovation, Novel,
Unprecedented

Sound & Hearing

Acoustics, Cacophony,
Clamor, Din, Discordant,
Euphony, Mellifluous,
Raucous, Strident, Vociferous

Cheapness or Care in Spending

Austere, Avaricious, Frugal,
Mercenary, Miserly,
Parsimonious, Penurious,
Thrifty

Respect & Praise

Acclaim, Accolade, Adulate,
Esteem, Eulogize, Exalt, Extol,
Laud, Panegyrize, Revere,
Venerate

Stubborn

Adamant, Dogmatic,
hidebound, Intractable,
Obdurate, Obstinate,
Recalcitrant, Resolve,
Unwavering, Unyielding,
Willful

Passion & Enthusiasm

Ardent, Avid, Ebullient,
Effervescent, Exuberant,
Fanatical, Fervent,
Impassioned, Vibrant, Zealous

Generosity & Concern

Altruistic, Benevolent,
Largess, Lavish,
Magnanimous, Munificent,
Philanthropic, Prodigal,
Squander

Fighting & Bad Feelings

Animosity, Antagonism,
Bellicose, Belligerent,
Cantankerous, Captious,
Contentious, Disputatious,
Polemical, Predator,
Pugnacious

Friendly & Agreeable

Affable, Amiable, Amicable,
Congenial, Convivial, Cordial,
Gregarious, Jocular, Levity

Making Things Better

Allay, Alleviate, Ameliorate,
Appease, Assuage, Conciliate,
Mediate, Mitigate, Mollify,
Pacify, Placate, Quell

Ways of Speaking

Bombastic, Circumlocution,
Colloquial, Diffuse, Digress,
Eloquence, Garrulous,
Grandiloquent, Loquacious,
Prattle, Ramble, Rant,
Rhetorical, Verbose, Voluble

Mean or Harmful

Baneful, Deleterious,
Detrimental, Devious,
Iniquitous, Malicious,
Nefarious, Odious, Ominous,
Pernicious, Rancorous,
Virulent

No Interest or Emotion

Aloof, Apathetic, Detached,
Impassive, Indifferent,
Listless, Nonchalant,
Phlegmatic, Remote, Stolid

Obedience & Humility

Compliant, Fawning,
Obsequious, Servile, Slavish,
Submissive, Subordinate,
Subservient, Sycophant,
Toady

Food & Hunger

Abstemious, Alimentary,
Culinary, Delectable,
Emaciated, Epicurean,
Glutton, Palatable, Ravenous,
Savory, Voracious

Brief in Time or Place

Ephemeral, Evanescent,
Fleeting, Itinerant, Nomadic,
Peripatetic, Transient,
Transitory, Volatile

Sneaky or Secret

Clandestine, Covert, Furtive,
Inconspicuous, Sly, Stealthy,
Surreptitious, Unobtrusive

Not Important

Extraneous, Frivolous,
Incidental, Inconsequential,
Irrelevant, Negligible,
Peripheral, Petty, Superficial,
Trifling, Trivial

Smart or Wise

Acute, Astute, Discerning,
Erudite, Incisive, Ingenious,
Judicious, Perspicacious,
Prudent, Sagacious, Savvy,
Shrewd

Small Amount

Dearth, Deplete, Devoid,
Paucity, Scarcity, Sparse

Get Rid Of

Abolish, Abrogate, Annihilate, Annul, Efface, Eradicate, Expunge, Nullify, Obliterate, Vanquish, Void

High Point

Acme, Apex, Apogee, Peak,
Pinnacle, Summit, Zenith

Rest

Cessation, Hiatus, Lull,
Moratorium, Reprieve,
Respite, Siesta

Frustrate or Prevent

Baffle, Deter, Foil, Hamper,
Hinder, Impede, Obstruct,
Preclude, Stymie, Thwart

Lie

Embellish, Embroider,
Equivocate, Fabricate,
Prevaricate

Flexible

Agile, Elastic, Limber, Lithe,
Nimble, Pliant, Supple

Beginner

Amateur, Apprentice,
Fledgling, Neophyte, Novice,
Rookie, Tyro

Confuse

Baffle, Befuddle, Bemuse,
Bewilder, Confound, Perplex

Literary Terms You Should Know

Allusion: passing reference or indirect mention

Anecdote: short account of an incident (especially a biographical one)

Catharsis: purging of emotional tension

Euphemism: inoffensive expression substituted for an offensive one

Hyperbole: extravagant exaggeration

Irony: incongruity between what might be expected and what occurs

Metaphor: a figure of speech that suggests a non-literal similarity not using "Like" or "As"

Oxymoron: conjoining contradictory terms (as in Jumbo Shrimp)

Parable: a short moral story

Parody: a composition that imitates or misrepresents somebody's style, usually in a humorous way

Pathos: a quality that arouses emotions, especially pity or sorrow

Prose: ordinary writing as distinguished from verse

Satire: witty language used to convey insults or scorn

Vignette: a brief literary description

Good Luck!

Good luck!

Made in United States
Orlando, FL
01 July 2023

34688075R00068